CONTENTS

ROMAN BRITAIN

Two thousand years ago the city of Rome was at the centre of a great empire. Year by year the empire grew, as the Roman army conquered more lands. In AD 43, the Romans came to conquer Britain.

The people who lived in Britain at that time were called Britons or Celts. Each family belonged to a tribe and the tribe was led by a king or queen. The British tribes tried to fight off the Roman army but most of them were soon defeated.

The Romans began to make Britain more like the rest of their empire. They built towns, with roads to link them. The Britons had never lived in towns. They had always lived on farms. At first they hated the Romans but soon some Britons began to copy them.

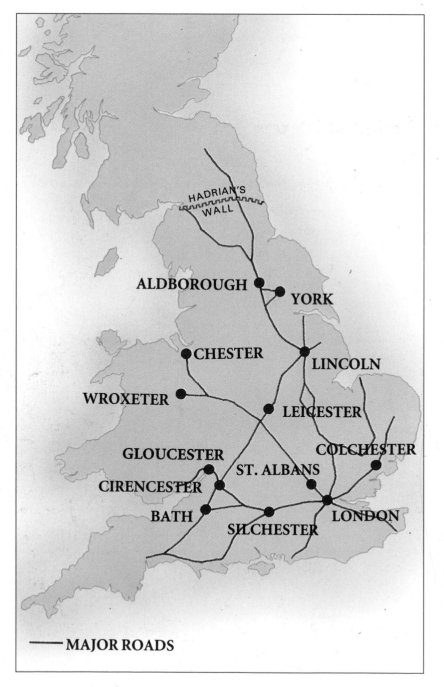

HADRIAN'S WALL

ALDBOROUGH

YORK

CHESTER

LINCOLN

WROXETER

LEICESTER

GLOUCESTER

COLCHESTER

ST. ALBANS

CIRENCESTER

BATH

SILCHESTER

LONDON

— MAJOR ROADS

▲ This map shows the main towns and roads that the Romans built in Britain.

WHAT FAMILIES WERE LIKE

ROMAN BRITAIN

ALISON COOPER

an imprint of Hodder Children's Books

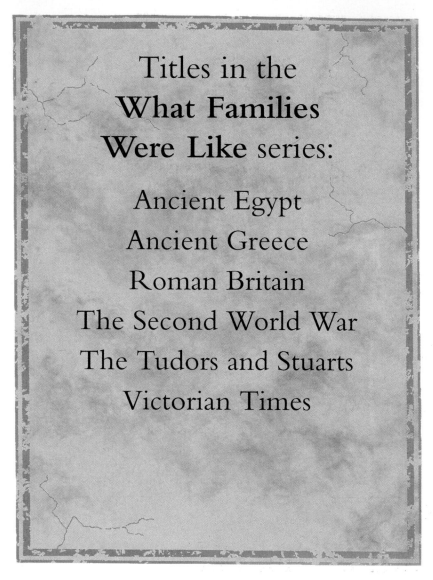

Titles in the
**What Families
Were Like** series:

Ancient Egypt

Ancient Greece

Roman Britain

The Second World War

The Tudors and Stuarts

Victorian Times

This book is a simplified version of the book *Roman Britain*
in Hodder Wayland's 'Family Life' series.
Text copyright © 2001 Hodder Wayland
Volume copyright © 2001 Hodder Wayland
First published in 2001 by Hodder Wayland, an imprint of Hodder Children's Books.
This paperback edition published in 2003

Language level consultant: Norah Granger
Editor: Belinda Hollyer
Designer: Jane Hawkins

British Library Cataloguing in Publication Data
Cooper, Alison
What families were like – Roman Britain
1.Family – Great Britain – History – Juvenile literature
2.Romans – Great Britain – Social life and customs
I.Title II.Roman Britain
936.2'04
ISBN 0-7502-4446-1

Printed in Hong Kong by Wing King Tong

Hodder Children's Books
A division of Hodder Headline Limited
338 Euston Road, London NW1 3BH

Picture acknowledgements:
Cover: Bronze brooch, family Lar (god) & back cover ring British Museum
Trustees, chariot race mosaic © Hull City Council, background mosaic Pergamon
Museum, Berlin, Germany/Bridgeman Art Library; Ancient Art & Architecture
Collection 8 (right), 10 (top), 12 (top), 14 (both), 17, 25 (right), 28 (bottom);
Audio-Visual Centre 21 (top), 25 (top); Bath Archaeological Trust 12 (bottom), 26
(bottom); City Museum and Art Gallery, Carlisle 11; Colchester Museums 15
(right) 28 (top); County Council and Bignor Villa 19 (top); English Heritage 23
(top), 27 (bottom); Hull City Museums and Art Galleries 29 (top); Museum of
Antiquities of the University & Society of Antiquities of Newcastle upon Tyne 7
(right); Museum of London 13 (top), 21 (bottom); The National Museum of
Wales 29 (bottom); National Trust 19; Reading Museum and Art Gallery 23
(bottom); St Albans Museums 20; Trustees of the British Museum 10 (bottom), 16,
22, 27 (top); Yorkshire Museum 7 (left), 8 (left), 15 (left).
All artwork is by Peter Dennis except 6 (Jenny Hughes).

Wealthy Britons learnt to speak Latin, which was the Roman language. They began to dress like Romans too, and built houses in the Roman style. Life for poor Britons did not change very much. They carried on farming their land.

▲ The Britons lived on farms like this, called homesteads.

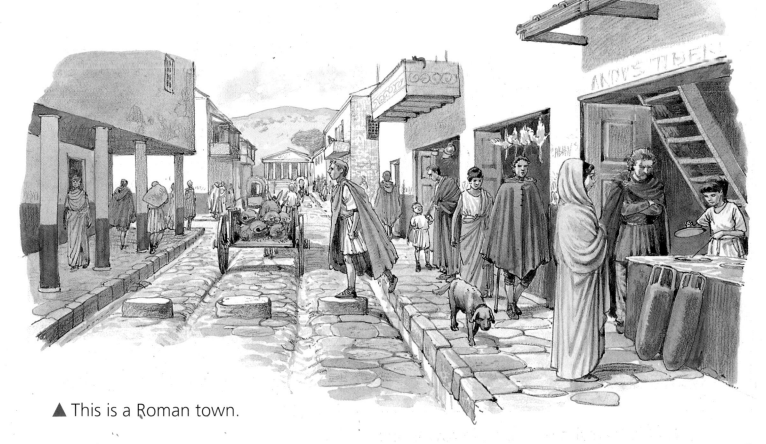

▲ This is a Roman town.

The people of Roman Britain

People from many different countries lived in Roman Britain. The soldiers in the Roman army came from Greece, France, Spain, North Africa, Italy and Syria. Many of these men stayed in Britain and married local women. Women from northern Europe were brought to Britain to work as slaves. Some married British men after they were freed from slavery.

The countries that are coloured yellow on this map were part of the Roman empire in AD 117. That was the time when the empire was at its biggest. ▼

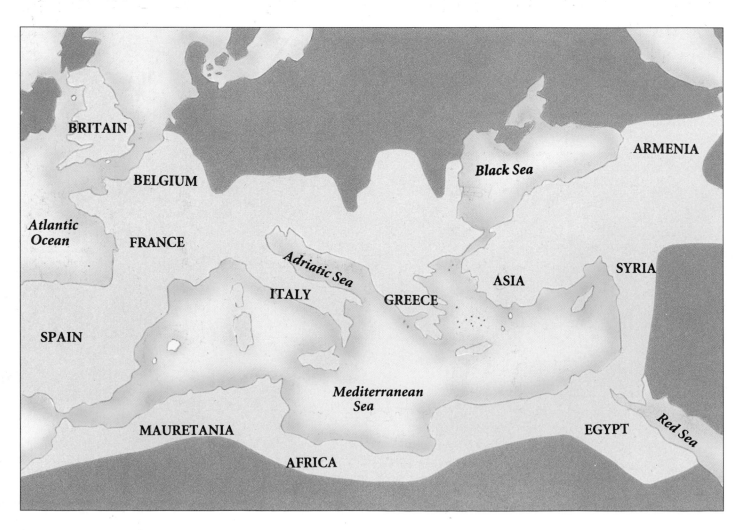

People also came to Britain to buy and sell goods. The picture on the right shows a tombstone. It was set up by a merchant from Syria, in memory of his wife. She was a British woman but she wore Roman clothes and had a Roman name – Regina. She spoke Celtic and her husband spoke a language called Palmyrene. Luckily they were able to speak to each other in Latin! The Roman language and the Roman way of life kept all these different peoples together.

This is Regina's tombstone. Regina means 'queen' in Latin. ▼

◄ This is the tombstone of a smith. He was rich enough to afford a carved tombstone. Craftsmen like him did well when the Romans ruled Britain.

7

FAMILIES

Before the Romans came, people in Britain lived in big family groups. Parents, grandparents, aunts and uncles lived together on one homestead. They all helped to run the farm and look after the children. Women were important. Some of them were queens who ruled tribes.

▲ This tombstone shows a woman called Julia Velva, with her family around her.

This kind of statue is called a bust. Wealthy families had busts made showing their fathers and grandfathers. ▶

Roman families

Roman families were different. The Romans lived in small family groups. The most important person in the family was the oldest man. He was called the *Pater Familias* (father of the family). Everyone else had to obey him.

Men expected their wives to look after the home. This is what the Emperor Augustus said about wives:

'What can be better than a wife who stays at home, manages the house for you and brings up your children; who gives you joy when you are well and comfort when you are sick…'

Men wanted their wives to have children. They could divorce a wife who could not have them. When a baby was on the way they hoped it would be a boy, because the Romans thought boys were more useful and valuable than girls.

This picture shows a Roman family in their dining room. ▼

Weddings

Girls did not usually decide who they wanted to marry. Their fathers chose a husband for them. Before the wedding the groom often gave a ring to the bride. She wore it on the same finger that people wear wedding rings on today.

The wedding took place at the bride's house. The couple held hands and promised to live together as husband and wife. The bride's father gave the groom some money called a dowry. If the groom divorced his wife later, he had to give the money back.

▲ This carving from Italy shows a couple getting married. You can see that they are holding hands.

Brides wore rings like these. You can see pictures of clasped hands on the right hand ring. ▶

10

Married life

Women usually got married between the ages of 18 and 28. Often their husbands were much older than them. Soldiers, for example, did not usually get married until they retired from the army. They were over 40 by then.

Rich women spent their time looking after the children and making sure the servants did their jobs properly. They also worked hard at their spinning. Poor women helped their husbands at work, out in the fields or in their workshops.

This carving shows a rich woman looking after her child. The child is playing with a pet bird. The woman is cooling herself with a fan. ▶

Clothes and hairstyles

Rich women in Roman Britain wore long tunics made from linen and silk. They coloured them with bright dyes. They liked to look fashionable. They looked at pictures of the Empress on coins and copied her hairstyle. They used perfume and make-up too. To make their lips and cheeks red they rubbed them with red wine.

Men looked at coins to find out what the emperor looked like. Emperor Hadrian had a beard, so lots of men copied him.

▲ This coin shows the Emperor Nero with his mother, Agrippina.

◄ The woman in this carving has a very complicated hairstyle. She might have curled her hair with tongs, or she could be wearing a wig.

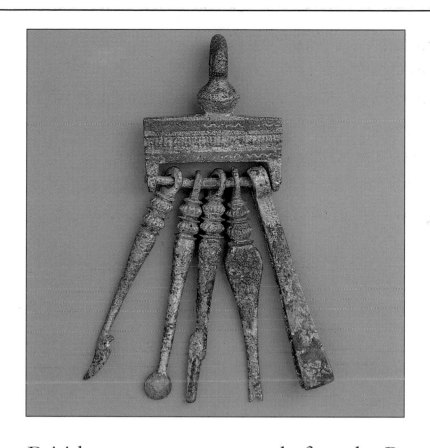

◄ This is a Roman manicure set. There is a nail file and a tool for cleaning the nails.

This picture shows the clothes Roman Britons wore. Men and women wore cloaks over their tunics to keep them warm. ▼

British men wore trousers before the Romans came. Later they copied the Romans and wore knee-length tunics. Men who were Roman citizens were allowed to wear a toga. This was a large piece of white cloth which they draped around themselves.

Lessons

In rich families, mothers or a family slave taught the young children how to read and write. They practised their writing on wooden boards covered with wax. They scratched letters into the wax with a pointed metal stick called a stylus.

Older boys went to school. Girls learned skills such as spinning and weaving at home. They learned how to dance and play music too.

Poor children did not have lessons. They began helping their parents with their work when they were very young.

▲ This is a wooden board and stylus, which children used for writing.

This carving shows a blacksmith at work. His children are helping him. ▶

14

▲ There is a picture of a family on this tombstone. The children are holding balls.

Playing games

All children enjoyed playing. They played with dolls made of wood or cloth, and with toy animals. Some of these toys have been found, so we know what they looked like. Children also played games such as leap frog and ball games.

These small models are children's toys. They were found in a child's grave in Colchester. ▶

Slaves

Rich families in Roman Britain had slaves to work for them. Slaves did not get paid for their work and they could not leave their job if they did not like it. They were owned by the family they worked for.

Slaves were often people who had been captured in wars. Some children were slaves because their parents had sold them to a slave owner!

This small bronze jar is in the shape of a sleeping boy slave. ▼

▲ In this picture two slaves are arranging their mistress's hair and another is holding up a mirror for her.

Slaves helped their owners to bathe and dress. Women slaves did the housework and helped to look after the children. Male slaves did jobs in the house, too, and looked after the garden or farm. Some slaves were educated and they taught the children.

Owners sometimes set free slaves who worked well for them. Freed slaves could set up their own shops or farms. They bought slaves of their own to help them.

AT HOME

Ordinary people lived in houses built of wattle. Wattle is twigs woven together to make strong walls. The wattle was covered with daub (clay). Rich people's homes were built of stone. They were often built in the shape of a rectangle, with a courtyard in the middle.

Rich Roman Britons lived in houses like this one. ▼

▲ This is a mosaic from a Roman villa (a large country house) at Bignor in Sussex.

Living in luxury

Some rich people decorated the floors of their homes with mosaics. A mosaic is a picture made up of thousands of tiny coloured tiles. Under the floor they sometimes had a heating system. It was called a hypocaust. The floors were raised up on brick columns. Hot air from a fire went under the floor and warmed the rooms above.

This picture shows the remains of a hypocaust at Chedworth Roman villa. You can see the columns that held the floor. ▶

Food

Today oysters are a luxury food but in Roman Britain they were very common. Even poor people could afford to eat them. We know that Roman Britons ate many different birds too, such as swans, gulls, and even thrushes and jackdaws. The bones of these birds have been found in Roman rubbish pits.

The Romans brought new herbs and spices to Britain, such as mint and mustard. They also brought olive oil and a spicy fish sauce called garum. The Romans loved garum and put it on lots of different dishes.

▲ These pots and bowls were found at St Albans. You can also see some of the food that people ate in Roman times.

This is a Roman kitchen that has been set up in the Museum of London. On the right you can see a pot being heated on the fire. ▶

These objects were used to warm and serve wine. ▼

Before the Romans came to Britain, people's main drink was beer made from barley. Later, rich Britons copied the Romans and drank wine. Some wine was made from grapes grown in southern Britain. Most of it was brought from France in tall pottery jars called amphorae.

The Romans ate their main meal in the late afternoon or early evening (look back to page 9 to see a picture of a family eating). They used knives to cut up their food but they did not have forks. They used their fingers instead.

Household gods

The Romans believed that every house had its own gods. A god called the Lar protected all the members of the family. Gods called the Penates looked after the family's food. Each family kept small statues of the household gods in a shrine. Every day the women put flowers or food on the shrine, to please the gods.

This is the statue of a family Lar. He is often shown as a young dancing man. ▶

▲ In this picture you can see a board used for playing 'soldiers'. You can also see some dice, cups for shaking them, and some playing pieces.

Games and music

People enjoyed playing dice, and board games. The board in the picture above was used for a game called soldiers. It was a bit like draughts. Each player tried to capture the other players' pieces by surrounding them.

Families also enjoyed music and dancing. The women were often the best musicians. They played pipes and stringed instruments called lyres. In the evenings they entertained the rest of the family with their music.

▲ This statue shows a young woman holding a tibia. A tibia was a flute made from a hollow plant.

TOWN LIFE

Roman towns looked much the same wherever they were in the empire. They all had a big square forum, temples and bath-houses. This picture shows the main buildings in a Roman town.

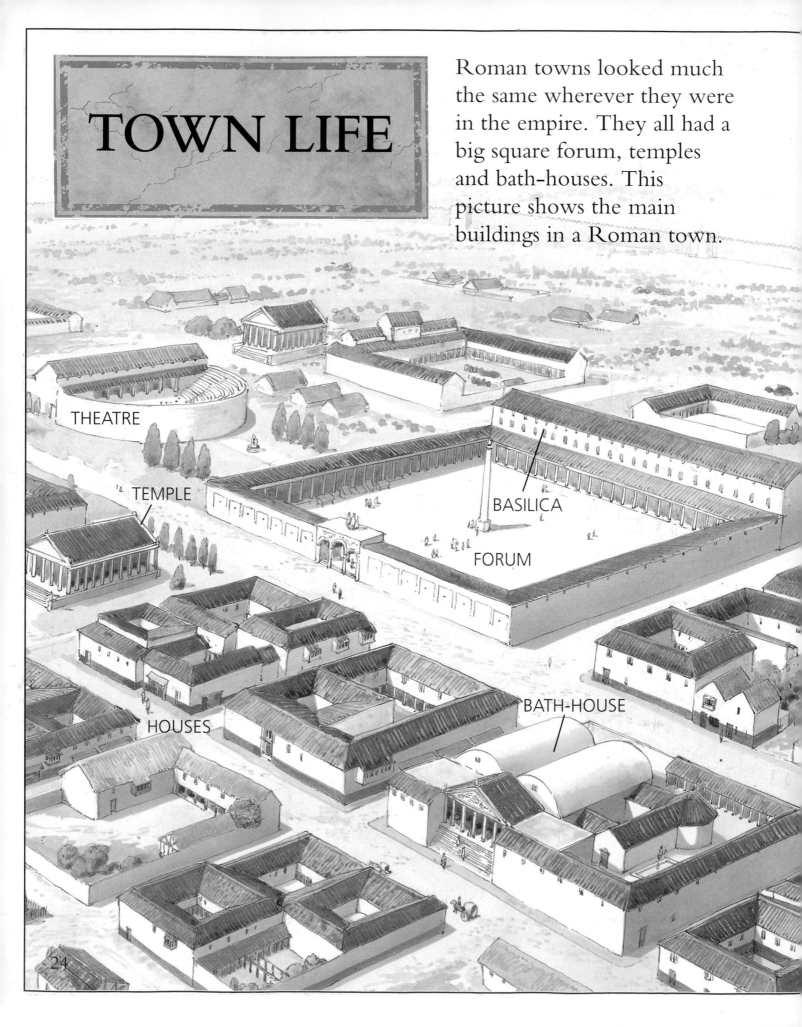

THEATRE

TEMPLE

BASILICA

FORUM

HOUSES

BATH-HOUSE

The forum and basilica

Shoppers crowded around market stalls in the centre of the forum. Men went to town council meetings in the basilica. This was a large hall on one side of the forum. It was also used as a lawcourt.

This is a ruined temple. The god Mithras was worshipped here. ▼

▲ Priestesses like this one gave gifts to the gods.

Temples

In every Roman town there were several temples. Ordinary people took gifts to the temples and asked the gods and goddesses to help them. For example, one man in Norfolk asked the god Neptune to punish a thief who had stolen some money from him.

Furnace

Very hot room

Hot room

Warm room

Cold room

▲ This diagram shows the different rooms in the bath-house. The hottest room was the one nearest the furnace.

A visit to the baths

The Roman baths were a bit like a modern leisure centre. People liked to meet their friends there. Before their bath they could do some exercise in the courtyard.

Inside the baths there were several rooms. In the hot room, people sat and sweated. Slaves massaged them with olive oil. Then the slaves scraped away the oil and dirt with a curved metal tool called a strigil. In another room the bathers enjoyed a soak in warm water. Finally, they took a refreshing dip in the cold water room.

◀ In a town called Bath, the Roman baths were filled with water from a spring. This water was already hot when it came out of the ground.

Toilets

The Romans laid pipes to carry the water from springs and rivers to their bath-houses. They also used running water to flush their toilets. In the public toilets people sat side by side. There were no separate cubicles. They used small bits of sponge on sticks instead of toilet paper.

▲ In this picture you can see two strigils and a pot used for olive oil.

These are the ruins of a Roman toilet, at Housesteads fort in Northumberland. Twenty men could use this toilet at the same time. ▶

Theatres

There were theatres in the important towns in Roman Britain, such as Colchester, Canterbury and St Albans. The theatres did not have roofs. They were open to the sky. People enjoyed comedies (funny plays) and tragedies (sad plays). The actors wore wooden masks to show the sort of character they were playing.

▲ This vase shows a fight between two gladiators. Gladiators were slaves or criminals who were forced to fight.

You can still see the outline of the Roman theatre here at St Albans. ▼

▲ This mosaic shows a chariot race.

Fights and races

The amphitheatre looked a bit like a football stadium. In the centre, gladiators fought each other to the death. Sometimes they battled with fierce animals such as bears.

Roman Britons also loved watching chariot races. Each chariot belonged to a different team. The crowd cheered on their teams as the chariots rushed around the race track.

◀ Actors' masks looked like this. This is not a real mask – it is a copy carved in stone.

GLOSSARY

AD This stands for 'Anno Domini' which is Latin for 'in the year of our Lord'. The years before Christ was born are called 'BC' ('Before Christ') and the years from his birth onwards are called 'AD'.

Celtic (Pronounced 'keltic') The language of the Celts, a people who lived in Britain and northern Europe.

Chariot A light wagon with two wheels, pulled by a horse. The driver rode in it standing up.

Citizen A Roman citizen was a man who had the right to vote.

Column A thick pole that holds up a roof (or a floor in a hypocaust).

Conquered Beaten in a war and taken over by an enemy.

Courtyard An open space surrounded by walls or buildings.

Dyes Chemicals used to colour cloth. In Roman times they were often made from plant juices.

Empire Many countries which are ruled by one king or emperor.

Furnace A very hot fire.

Merchant Someone who buys and sells large amounts of goods.

Roman Britons People who were British, or who had British fathers and grandfathers, but copied the Roman way of life.

Shrine A shelf or a special place on the wall (a bit like a cupboard), where families left gifts for the gods.

Slaves Workers who did not get paid. The person they worked for owned them, and could sell them to someone else.

Smith Somebody who makes objects from metal.

Spinning Twisting and pulling pieces of wool to make it into threads.

Spring A place where water bubbles up from under the ground.

Temple A building where people worship a god or goddess.

Tribe A group made up of several families who live in a particular area.

Tunic A type of clothing. It was a bit like a dress, fastened with a belt around the waist.

Weaving Linking threads together to make cloth.

Books to read

Emperors, Gladiators and other jobs for Ancient Romans by Anita Ganeri (Heinemann Library, 1997)

Women in Ancient Rome by Fiona Macdonald (Belitha, 2000)

You wouldn't want to be a Roman Gladiator by John Malam (Hodder Wayland, 2000)

Places to visit

Arbeia Roman Fort, Baring Street, South Shields, Tyne and Wear.
This is one of the forts of Hadrian's Wall. The museum has some of the best Roman British carved tombstones, including that of Regina, shown on page 7.

Bath Roman Museum, Abbey Churchyard, Bath, Avon.
This includes the famous Roman baths.

Bignor Roman Villa, near Arundel, West Sussex.
This has beautiful mosaics, such as the picture of Venus on page 19.

Corinium Museum, Park Street, Cirencester, Gloucestershire.
This museum has Roman sculpture, mosaics and reconstructions of a kitchen and a dining room.

Fishbourne Roman Palace, Salthill Road, near Chichester, West Sussex.
This palace is thought to be the great palace of the British King Cogidubnus. It has fine mosaics and a replanted Roman garden.

Verulamium Museum, St Albans, Hertfordshire.
St Albans was the third largest Roman city in Britain. In the museum you can see objects found in the ruins of the city. Nearby, you can visit a Roman theatre.

INDEX